First published in Great Britain 1977 by Ward Lock Ltd.
Copyright © 1977 by Grisewood & Dempsey Ltd.
All rights reserved. a b c d e f g h
This edition is published by Derrydale, a division of
Crown Publishers, Inc.
Printed in Singapore by Tien Wah Press (Pte) Ltd.

Library of Congress Cataloging in Publication Data

Kilpatrick, Cathy.
   Let's look at the seashore.

   Includes index.
   SUMMARY: An introduction to life at the edge of the
sea in both warm and cold climates.
   1. Seashore biology--Juvenile literature.
2. Marine biology--Juvenile literature. [1. Seashore
biology. 2. Marine biology] I. Allen, Graham,
1940- II. Justice, Jennifer. III. Title.
QH95.7.K54 1979   574.909'4'6   79-84395
ISBN 0-517-28727-7

LET'S LOOK AT
THE SEASHORE

Written by Cathy Kilpatrick

Illustrated by Graham Allen

Edited by Jennifer Justice

DERRYDALE · NEW YORK

Beaches and Shores

A seashore often looks empty and still. Apart from the sea itself, nothing seems to move. But this area is home to many different living things. Some are tiny creatures too small for the human eye to see without using a microscope. Others are large animals, such as conger eels, octopuses, polar bears and seals.

There are many different kinds of seashore. Some are huge, bare stretches of sand. Others are rocky. When the tide is out, pools of water full of seaweed and animals are left behind in the rocks. There are also mud and shingle shores, and even shores made up entirely of seashells.

The seashore is a changing home for the animals and plants that live there. Twice a day when the tide comes in, they are in salt water. Then, when the tide

This picture shows several kinds of seashore. The cliffs provide good nesting places for many sea birds. Below the cliffs on the left is a rocky shore with pools of sea water left behind by the tide. There is a shingle beach on the right.

Land plants such as thrift grow near the water. Strong grass grows on top of the sand dunes. These are great heaps of sand, blown up from the sandy part of the shore. Muddy shores occur where rivers and streams flow into the sea. Birds search the mud and sand for animals that live beneath the surface.

cliffs

thrift

herring gull

rock pool

6

goes out, they are left in the open. The sun may dry them out; low temperatures may freeze them. During storms, waves whipped up by the wind pound them with sand and stones.

The creatures of the shore have ways of surviving these changes. Being out of the water is dangerous for animals such as lugworms and sea urchins that can breathe only in water. So they bury themselves in the sand when the tide goes out. Other creatures, such as barnacles and periwinkles, have shells to keep water in and the sun out. Still others live undisturbed in the rock pools that stay behind when the tide goes out.

Some sea animals, like turtles and seals, come onto the seashore to breed. The young animals start life on land, but soon make the sea their home.

black-headed gull

shingle beach

sand dunes

sandy beach

stream

oystercatcher

mud beach

curlew

7

Life in the Sand

Many shore animals can breathe only in water. At high tide they live on or under the sand. When the tide goes out, enough water stays in the tiny spaces between the grains of sand to keep them alive. These animals all have special ways of moving into and through the sand.

The burrowing starfish uses its tube feet to dig itself deep into the sand. This starfish feeds on mollusks such as cockles. It takes a whole cockle, complete with shell, into its stomach. When the cockle opens its two shells slightly, special juices from the starfish's stomach flow into the cockle. These juices kill and digest the cockle's soft body.

The goose-foot star is so named because its shape is similar to the webbed foot of a goose. It does not dig itself very deep into the sand. Often it can be found lying on the surface of the sand. It lives on shrimps and mollusks.

oarweed

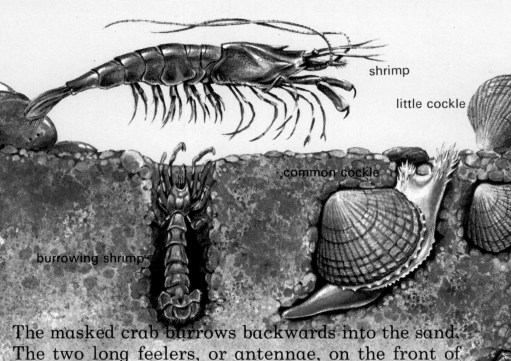

shrimp

shore crab

little cockle

common cockle

goose-foot star

burrowing shrimp

antennae

masked crab

The masked crab burrows backwards into the sand. The two long feelers, or antennae, on the front of its head form a tube up to the surface. This allows water to run down the tube so the crab can breathe while it is buried in the sand.

The common cockle lives on sandy beaches. It has a strong foot with which it can move along the beach and bury itself in the sand. At high tide, it breathes and feeds by pushing two tubes above the sand into the water.

burrowing starfish

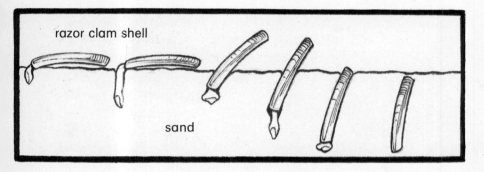

razor clam shell

sand

The razor clam goes below the sand when the tide is out. It stretches its muscular foot into the sand and pulls its shell behind it until it is quite hidden. The picture above shows how the razor clam digs itself into the sand.

When the tide goes out on sandy or muddy beaches, you may see hundreds of little coils of mud on the surface. These are made by the lugworm, which lives in a U-shaped burrow under the sand. It feeds by swallowing sandy mud that has scraps of plants and dead animals in it. The worm digests the food, and the sandy mud passes out onto the surface. This forms the coils, called worm casts. Fishermen often dig up lugworms to use as bait.

The amphitrite is a long worm that burrows into sandy mud. At one end of its body is a mass of tentacles. When the tide is in these tentacles wave about and bits of food in the water stick to them. Tiny hairs move the food down the tentacles to the amphitrite's mouth.

The purple heart urchin and the sea potato are two kinds of sea urchin that burrow into sand. The sea potato uses its long tube feet to feed, breathe, and feel.

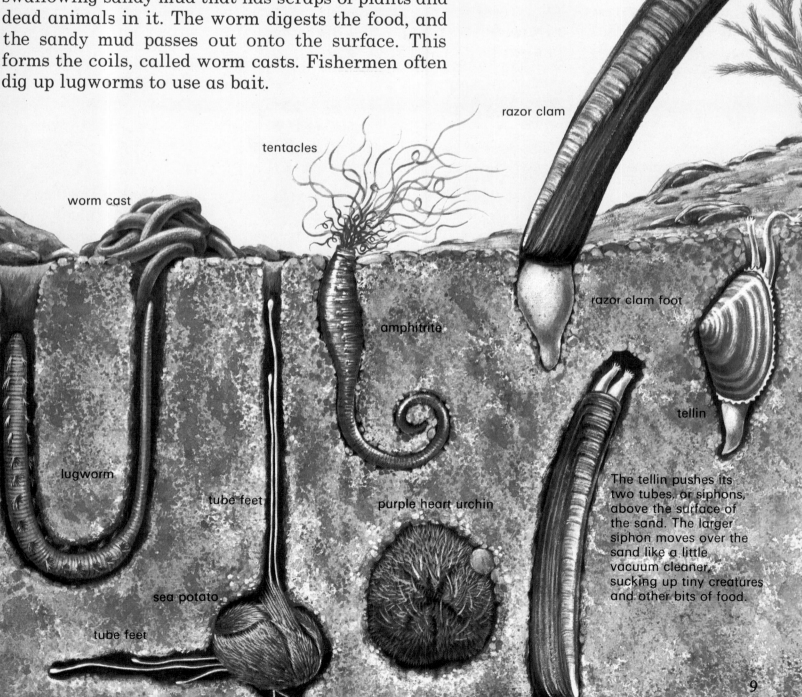

razor clam

tentacles

worm cast

amphitrite

razor clam foot

lugworm

tube feet

tellin

tube feet

sea potato

purple heart urchin

The tellin pushes its two tubes, or siphons, above the surface of the sand. The larger siphon moves over the sand like a little vacuum cleaner, sucking up tiny creatures and other bits of food.

9

All Kinds of Shells

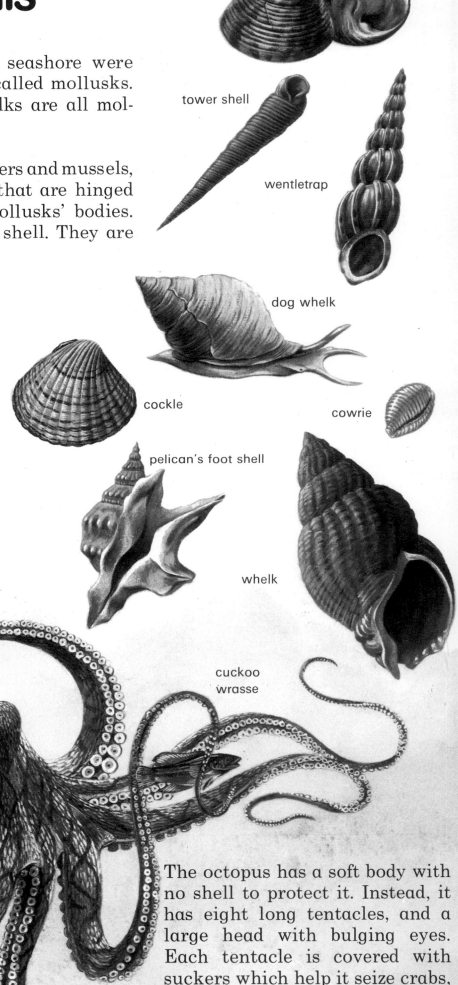

The empty shells you find on the seashore were once the homes of living animals called mollusks. Mussels, oysters, winkles and whelks are all mollusks; so are octopuses and squids.

Some mollusks, such as cockles, oysters and mussels, have a soft body inside two shells that are hinged together. The shells protect the mollusks' bodies. Other mollusks live inside a single shell. They are sometimes called "sea snails." The limpet has a cone-shaped shell. Underwater, the limpet moves on one large, fleshy foot.

Topshells, winkles, tower shells and whelks all have pretty coiled shells. Winkles, which are sometimes called periwinkles, like to live among the seaweeds they feed on. There is a picture of a periwinkle on page 15.

topshells

tower shell

wentletrap

dog whelk

cockle

cowrie

pelican's foot shell

whelk

scallop

octopus

cuckoo wrasse

The octopus has a soft body with no shell to protect it. Instead, it has eight long tentacles, and a large head with bulging eyes. Each tentacle is covered with suckers which help it seize crabs, lobsters, and other food. It pulls its prey into its beak-like jaws.

10

A limpet holds onto a rock with its strong foot. When the tide covers the limpet, it moves slowly over the rock, feeding on tiny plants. The limpet always returns to the same place on the rock. This soon leaves a mark in the shape of its shell.

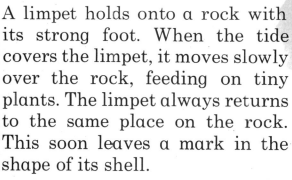

limpet

underside of limpet

slipper limpets

limpet's mark on rock

keyhole limpet

piddock

oval piddock

Piddocks can bore into soft rocks. A young piddock settles on a rock and its sucker-like foot holds its pointed shells against the rock. The piddock twists one way and then the other, and gradually bores its way into the rock.

Mussels live in large groups on rocks. Unlike a limpet, a mussel does not have a foot to hold it onto its rock. Instead, it produces a bundle of tough, sticky threads. These cling to the rock and firmly anchor the mussel.

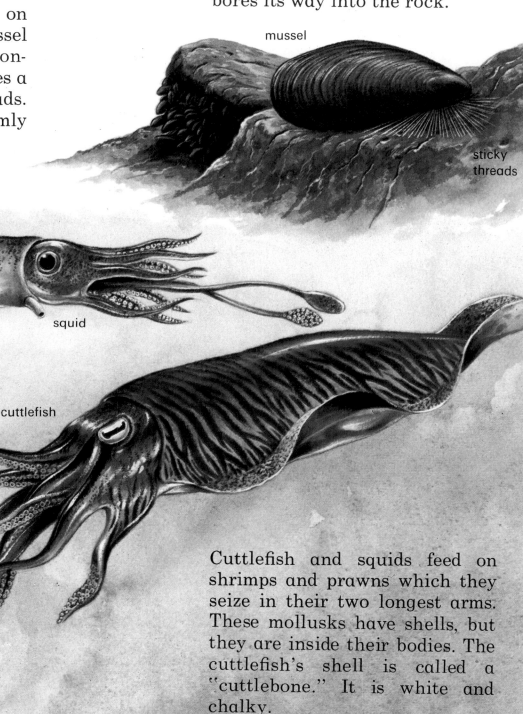

mussel

sticky threads

squid

cuttlefish

Cuttlefish and squids feed on shrimps and prawns which they seize in their two longest arms. These mollusks have shells, but they are inside their bodies. The cuttlefish's shell is called a "cuttlebone." It is white and chalky.

11

Birds of the Shore

The seashore provides food and good nesting places for many different types of bird. Some nest on cliffs; others among sand dunes. Many of the birds are waders with long legs. They find their food by probing the mud and water with their long beaks. Oystercatchers and avocets are wading birds. Other birds find their food in the sea. Some duck their heads underwater to catch fish. Some, like gannets, dive into the water from high in the air.

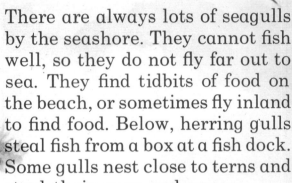

curlew

common tern

The male tern presents a fish to the female.

little terns

There are always lots of seagulls by the seashore. They cannot fish well, so they do not fly far out to sea. They find tidbits of food on the beach, or sometimes fly inland to find food. Below, herring gulls steal fish from a box at a fish dock. Some gulls nest close to terns and steal their eggs and young.

Terns nest in colonies. To attract a mate, a male tern flies over the colony with a fish in his bill, calling loudly. The female flies up in front of him and then they both settle on the ground. The male presents the fish to the female. After the birds have mated, they scrape a shallow nest in the sand. The female lays from one to three eggs, and both parents take turns to keep them warm. The chicks can leave the nest soon after hatching. If danger threatens, they stop moving and hug the ground. Because they are speckled grey and white they are very difficult to see against sand or pebbles.

herring gulls

gannet

young gannet

Most of the year, gannets spend hours gliding silently over the waves. But in the breeding season they screech and call over their huge nesting colonies on the cliffs. Gannets lay one egg each year, and both parents take turns at keeping it warm. When the chick hatches, it stays with its parents for about three months and then is left to look after itself.

oystercatchers

fulmar

puffin

Most birds of the shore have to be strong flyers because of the high winds over the sea. The fulmar's long, narrow wings are designed for gliding. It stays out at sea for months on end and hardly ever goes ashore except to breed.

The puffin has short wings and is not a strong flyer. It spends much of its time floating on the water. The oystercatcher is a noisy flyer. It makes shrill "kleep-kleep" calls as it flies.

Razorbills are expert divers and underwater swimmers. They chase fish underwater using their wings like paddles. They can dive to a depth of over 20 feet (6 meters) and can stay under the water for nearly a minute.

Razorbills often gather together and float on the water in huge "rafts." They then go through special courting actions, or displays. Some shake their heads from side to side. Others dive and then rise up from the water, their beaks pointing to the sky.

cormorant drying its wings

cormorants

razorbill

Cormorants are strong flyers but cannot fly very fast. They are the only web-footed birds that do not have waterproof oil on their feathers. After they dive for fish, they must land and stretch out their wings to dry. Cormorants eat more than their weight in fish each day.

13

In a Rock Pool

The rock pools on a seashore are exciting places to explore. A rock pool is sea water that is trapped in the rocks when the tide goes out. You can see many different animals swimming in the water or crawling among the seaweed on the rocks.

Sea anemones are strange animals that look like flowers. When the tide is in, they open up and wave their petal-like tentacles. The anemone uses its tentacles to catch food. Each tentacle is armed with hundreds of stinging cells. The stings from the cells stun any tiny fishes, shrimps or crabs that touch them. Then the tentacles push the helpless victim into the anemone's mouth, which is in the center of the ring of tentacles.

When the tide goes out, some anemones are left attached to rocks above the water of the pool. Their bodies are soft, like jelly. If they dry out, they die. To prevent this, each anemone closes up by pulling in its tentacles. There is enough water inside the anemone to keep it alive until the sea covers it again.

Seagulls often perch on the edge of rock pools, to feed on the creatures they find there. Here, a gull has seized a tiny crab to eat.

common gull

mussels

closed beadlet anemone

barnacles

topshells

dog whelk

anemone

prawn

edible sea urchin

crab

barnacle feeding

butterfish

starfish

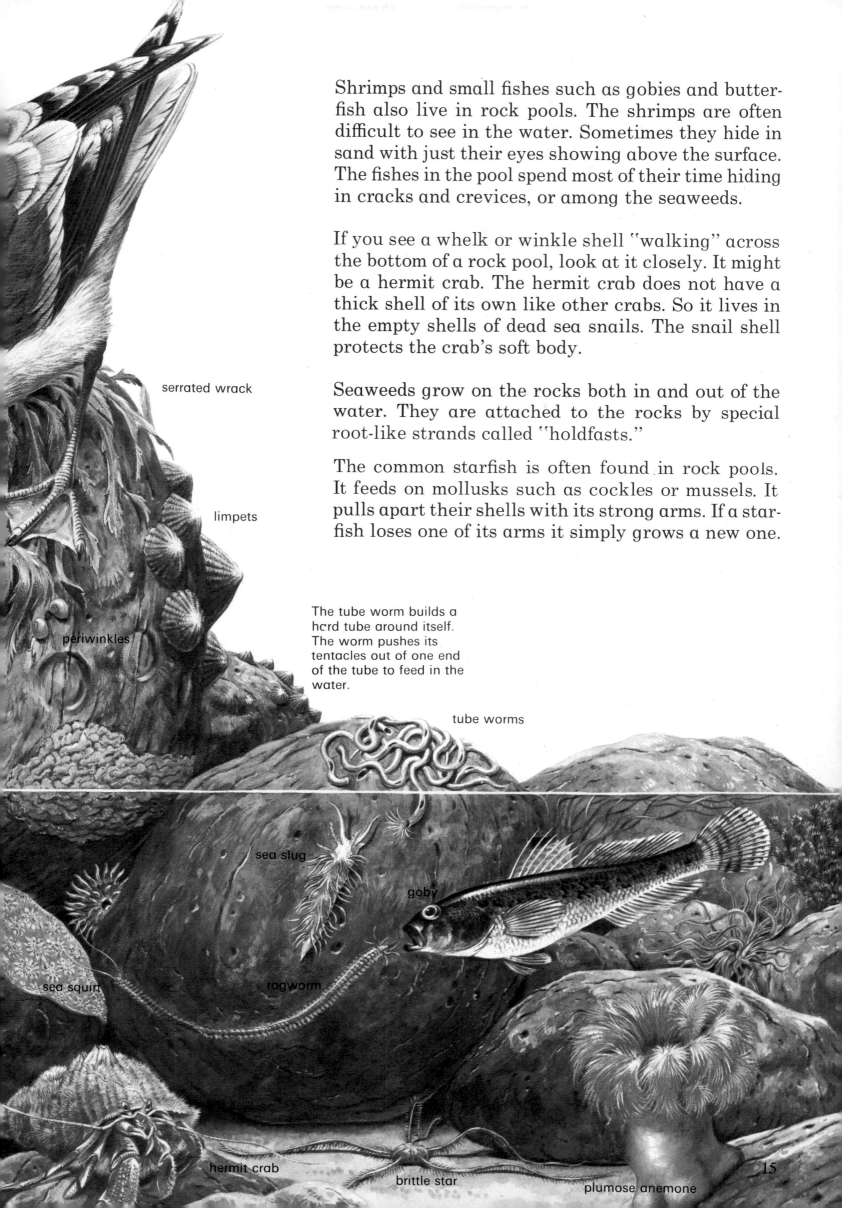

Shrimps and small fishes such as gobies and butter-fish also live in rock pools. The shrimps are often difficult to see in the water. Sometimes they hide in sand with just their eyes showing above the surface. The fishes in the pool spend most of their time hiding in cracks and crevices, or among the seaweeds.

If you see a whelk or winkle shell "walking" across the bottom of a rock pool, look at it closely. It might be a hermit crab. The hermit crab does not have a thick shell of its own like other crabs. So it lives in the empty shells of dead sea snails. The snail shell protects the crab's soft body.

Seaweeds grow on the rocks both in and out of the water. They are attached to the rocks by special root-like strands called "holdfasts."

The common starfish is often found in rock pools. It feeds on mollusks such as cockles or mussels. It pulls apart their shells with its strong arms. If a starfish loses one of its arms it simply grows a new one.

The tube worm builds a hard tube around itself. The worm pushes its tentacles out of one end of the tube to feed in the water.

serrated wrack

limpets

periwinkles

tube worms

sea slug

goby

sea squirt

ragworm

hermit crab

brittle star

plumose anemone

15

Crabs and Their Relatives

Crabs, lobsters, shrimps, prawns and barnacles all belong to a group of animals called crustaceans. Most of them have a hard shell or "crust," and several pairs of jointed legs, like insects. Many crustaceans live on or near the seashore.

Crabs live in the sea and along the shore in rock pools or under stones and seaweed. The shore crab is small, but it has strong claws for snapping up its prey. It is a very lively crab and, if disturbed, will scuttle away to find a new hiding place. The edible crab is much larger than the shore crab and its thick claws are much bigger. It lives near the shore in summer but goes farther out to sea in winter. Many people like to eat edible crabs.

When the hermit crab is small, it lives in a winkle shell. As it grows larger it finds larger shells to use. A fully grown hermit crab often uses a whelk shell as a home. It sometimes carries anemones and barnacles as "passengers" on its shell. As the crab feeds, the anemone's tentacles gather bits of the crab's leftover food. In return, the anemone's stinging cells may help to protect the crab from enemies such as octopuses and squids.

serrated wrack

anemone

sea lettuce

whelk shell

edible crab

sea spider

hermit crab

lobster

Shrimps and prawns look very much alike, but shrimps are smaller and flatter than prawns. They also have much larger front legs that end in hooks. Like many other crustaceans, shrimps and prawns are covered with hard, shell-like plates that protect them like armor. As they grow, they shed their old "suits" and grow new ones underneath.

Acorn barnacles look like little pointed hats stuck fast to the rocks. The hat is made of hard, strong plates. Inside them is a tiny shrimp-like animal. When a barnacle is under the water, the trapdoor which covers the top of the plates is open. The barnacle pushes out six pairs of bristly legs which trap tiny bits of food in the water. When the tide goes out and leaves the barnacle in the air, the door closes. There is enough water inside the barnacle's shell to keep it alive until the tide comes in again.

The lobster lives off rocky shores. It has five pairs of legs. The front pair of legs ends in large, strong pincers. The lobster uses these to seize and crush its prey. It can break the hard shell of a crab to get at the soft body inside. The lobster uses its four other pairs of legs to walk along the sea bottom.

The body of the goose barnacle is on the end of a long, thick stalk. It attaches itself by its stalk to the bottom of ships and buoys or to pieces of floating wood.

shore crab

ladder wrack

goose barnacles

prawn

The small, soft-bodied pea crab lives inside a mussel where it is safe. It strains tiny bits of food from the water inside the mussel shell.

The sea spider is a crab with a tiny body and long, spidery legs. It creeps slowly over the stones or seaweed.

serrated wrack

pea crab   mussels

shrimp

acorn barnacles

Shore Fishes

Many fishes swim close to the shore when the tide is in. But fishes can breathe only in water. Very few can stay near the shore when the tide goes out.

The greater sand eel and the common eel look more like snakes than fishes. Both are sometimes found along the shore. But the common eel's real home is in lakes and rivers. When it is time to breed, the eel makes an amazing journey. It travels thousands of miles from its freshwater home to the middle of the Atlantic Ocean. There the young eels, called elvers, are spawned. Only the elvers make the long journey back to the shores of North America and Europe. Then they swim up river and remain there until it is their turn to breed.

common eel

elvers

greater sand eel

shanny

sand goby

If you watch a rock pool long enough, you may see a shanny, or common blenny, darting about in the water. The blenny digs a shelter under a stone by wriggling its body in the gravel or sand. The male usually guards the eggs that the female lays. He fans his tail to keep the water moving around them. This helps them to get more air from the water.

The sand goby also guards its eggs until they hatch. It often hides under seaweeds.

Flatfishes such as flounders and plaice have both eyes on the same side of their bodies. This is because they lie on their sides on the sea floor. The flatfish is not born this way. As it grows, one eye gradually moves around its head until both eyes are on the same side. The flatfish's coloring matches the sand and pebbles on the sea floor, so its enemies cannot easily see it. When they are small, flatfishes often rest in the shallow waters near a sandy shore.

flounder

The Cornish sucker lives below the high tide mark, attached to the sides of stones. It clings with its sucker-like fins.

The butterfish is an eel-like blenny, and is so called because it is very slippery to handle. It often shelters among damp seaweeds when the tide is out.

The armed bullhead has a strange, upturned snout armed with spines. Bony plates on its body protect it like armor.

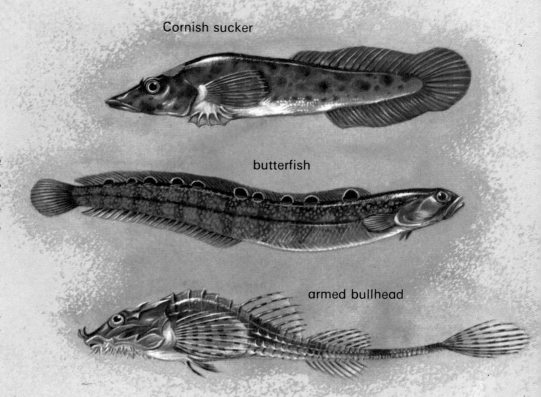

Cornish sucker

butterfish

armed bullhead

three-bearded rockling

angler fish

The three-bearded rockling lies quietly on the bottom of rock pools or under clumps of seaweed when the tide is out. It has three "whiskers" around its mouth that help it to feel for food in dark nooks and crannies.

The angler fish has its own fishing rod. Attached to its head is a special stalk with a tip that looks like a tasty worm. When the angler fish waves it slowly in the water, small fishes are attracted to the "worm." Before they know it, the angler fish has gobbled them up.

Seahorses and their relatives the pipefishes do not look like other fish. The seahorse's head looks a bit like the head of a horse. This fish swims in an upright position, and can wrap its tail around a piece of seaweed the way a monkey wraps its tail around a branch. The male seahorse has a pouch on his belly into which the female lays her eggs. For four or five weeks the male seahorse carries the eggs in his pouch until they hatch.

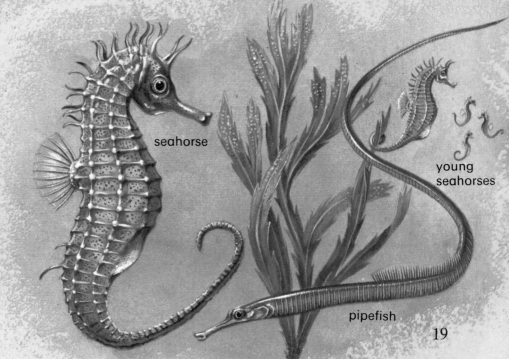

seahorse

young seahorses

pipefish

19

Sea Mammals

Many people think that whales, porpoises and dolphins are fish. But they are not. These animals are all mammals. Most mammals live on the land and all of them breathe air. Seals are also mammals that spend most of their time in the sea.

Once a year, gray seals must come ashore to have their young. A male seal is called a bull. He gathers several females together and guards them from other bulls. The group of females that "belongs" to one bull is called a "harem." When the females come ashore they are ready to have their pups.

The pups are born with a white woolly coat which they lose after a few weeks. They soon learn to swim and after about a month they are able to catch fish for themselves. Before the seals go back to the sea, the adults mate so that there will be more pups next year. Gray seals often stay close to a seashore all year round. They may even come up onto the beach or rocks in calm weather.

whalebone whale

close-up of whale's
jaws, showing baleen

The whalebone whale is a very large sea mammal but it eats only tiny animals. It strains thousands of them out of the water with strips of whalebone, called baleen, that hang down from the upper jaw of its huge mouth like the teeth of a comb.

A seal pup doubles its weight in the first two weeks of life by drinking its mother's rich milk. It becomes so fat and heavy that it can hardly move. Adult seals eat huge amounts of fish every day.

gray seal bull

gray seal pup

female gray seal

Seals are clumsy on land but are very graceful in the sea. The sleek body of the seal is perfectly shaped for swimming through the water. Its back feet are webbed like those of a duck. The seal holds them together and uses them in the water the way a fish uses its tail. They push the seal through the water. The seal's front limbs, or flippers, are also webbed. The seal uses them to steer underwater and to pull itself along the ground on land. It can also use them like hands to hold food as it eats.

Dolphins and porpoises are small whales. They often swim close to a seashore, feeding on small fishes. They have a smooth, streamlined body with a large fin on their backs. They do not stay underwater all the time. Like other mammals they have to come up to the surface for air.

The porpoise is very like a dolphin, but it has a more rounded snout and flippers. Porpoises live along coasts, and sometimes swim up rivers.

whale

Dolphins and porpoises are playful creatures. They leap right up out of the water, twisting this way and that and nudging one another with their snouts.

porpoise

common dolphin

common seal

gray seal

harp seal

21

Life in Cold Seas

The shores of the Arctic and Antarctic are bare, cold and icy. Yet many kinds of birds and mammals like to live there because there is always plenty of fish to eat. Each animal has its own way of surviving in the bitter cold, ice, and snow.

On the shores of the Antarctic live curious birds that cannot fly. These are penguins. The largest of all penguins is the emperor penguin. In March each bird comes ashore to find a mate. A month later the female of each pair lays a single egg. She passes it over to her mate to keep warm while she goes off to fish for food. The male penguin stands on the ice without eating for about 60 days until she returns to take over the job of keeping the egg warm. Soon the egg hatches. The female feeds the chick on fish that she brings up from her stomach.

In the frozen land around the North Pole the polar bear is master. It hunts and kills seals, baby walruses, birds and even arctic foxes. A female polar

The emperor penguin chick stays warm and safe between its parent's feet.

emperor penguin

penguin chicks

polar bear

The ptarmigan may be found along the Arctic shores all the year round. As the seasons change, its colors change. In autumn it grows white feathers. They protect the ptarmigan by making it difficult for enemies to see it against the white snow. In spring its white feathers are replaced by brownish ones which match the color of the ground in summer.

polar bear cubs

ptarmigan

bear gives birth to her cubs in the middle of winter in a snow cave. In spring when the cubs are stronger the family leaves its winter home.

The thick, heavy coat of the musk ox protects it from the cold in winter and from swarms of biting insects in summer. When danger threatens, a herd of musk oxen forms a circle, with the young in the middle. Each adult ox faces outward toward the enemy. Its large horns are a match for a polar bear or wolf.

Walruses live in large groups. They use their long tusks of ivory to rake clams and other shellfish from the sea bed. Their bristling moustaches strain the mud from their food. A walrus may eat hundreds of clams in one meal. A baby walrus depends mainly on its mother's rich milk for food until it is two years old. By this time its tusks have grown to about 4 inches (10 cm), and the young walrus can begin to dig for shellfish on its own.

Humpback whales often come close to the shore. They migrate to polar waters every summer to feed on tiny shrimp-like animals called krill.

A female snowy owl seizes a lemming in her strong claws.

female snowy owl

lemming

The snowy owl has white feathers which blend in with the winter landscape. Unlike the ptarmigan, it stays white with just a few dark spots all the year round. The female has more dark feathers than the male so that she cannot be seen easily on her nest in summer.

humpback whale

arctic foxes

musk ox calf

musk oxen

walrus

walrus pup

Life in Warm Seas

In the shallow seas of the warm parts of the world live large sea turtles. They spend their life in the water, but return to the land to lay their eggs. The turtles mate at sea. Then the females swim to the land, often to the same sandy beaches where they were born. Each turtle struggles slowly up the beach to a place above the high water mark. There she digs a hole about 1½ feet (half a meter) deep with her strong hind flippers. The female lays between 50 and 150 eggs in the hole. She can lay about 12 eggs a minute. When she has finished, she fills in the hole and smooths over the surface with her flippers.

Then the turtle makes her way slowly back to the sea. She leaves the eggs to hatch in the warm sun. After a while, the little turtles dig their way out of the sand. Each turtle knows exactly which way to crawl to get to the sea. But until they are in the water, the young turtles are in great danger. Many are eaten by sea birds, ghost crabs, and land animals that live near the shore. Even when they reach the water the little turtles are not completely safe. Many fall victim to crocodiles and sharks.

Above, from top to bottom: A young turtle begins to break out of the egg. Then it starts its journey through the sand to the open air. Several turtles climb out onto the sand at the same time. The gulls and frigate birds are waiting. As the little turtles scuttle away toward the sea, many are picked up and eaten by the birds.

turtle

Fiddler crabs live in large numbers on mud flats and swamps in warm places. Each crab has its own burrow in the mud and stays near it, keeping other crabs away. The male fiddler has one very large claw. But though the claw looks like a dangerous weapon, the crab does not often use it for defense. Instead, he waves it in the air to attract females or to frighten other male fiddlers away from the area around his burrow. A visitor to a fiddler crab colony will see a curious sight – hundreds of tiny crabs waving their large claws in the air.

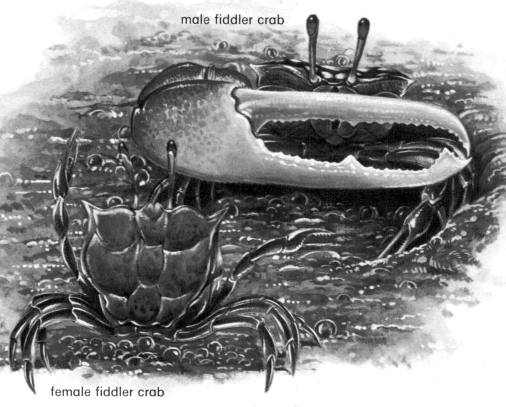
male fiddler crab

female fiddler crab

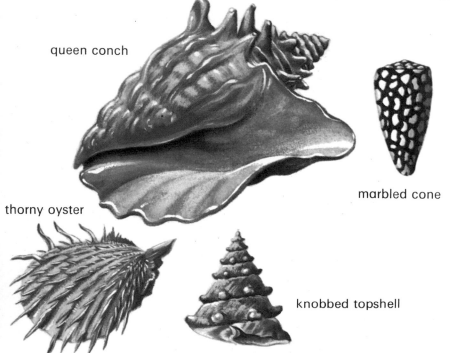
queen conch

marbled cone

thorny oyster

knobbed topshell

Many of the mollusks that live in warm seas have beautiful shells. They are often brightly colored and patterned. Some grow very large. The queen conch of the Caribbean Sea has a shell up to 12 inches (30 cm) long. The thorny oyster shell is covered with long spines. It is sometimes called a chrysanthemum shell because it looks rather like a chrysanthemum flower. The marbled cone lives in the sand along coral reefs. The knobbed topshell is one of more than 1000 different kinds of topshell.

mudskipper

Mudskippers live on mud flats and in mangrove swamps along the edge of the sea. When the tide goes out, the mudskippers stay behind on the muddy shore. They can breathe air and use their fins like legs to crawl and hop over the mud. Some mudskippers can even pull themselves up onto mangrove roots with special sucker-like fins. Their eyes are on little stalks, which helps them to see in all directions.

If danger threatens, mudskippers will hop, skip or jump away. Some go inland; others take to the water. They are very hard to catch.

The Coral Builders

Below the surface of some warm seas are great walls built entirely by tiny animals. These are called coral reefs. Corals are like small sea anemones. They build little stone "cups" around themselves to protect their soft bodies.

When the coral dies the stony skeleton is left behind. Young corals build their skeletons on top of the empty ones. Slowly the corals build up into a great wall, or reef. The largest coral reef in the world is the Great Barrier Reef of Australia. It is over 1250 miles (2000 km) long. Many beautiful and brightly colored fish live among the corals. Other sea creatures live hidden in the spaces between the lumps of coral. They come out at night to feed.

A coral reef is made up of many kinds of coral, of all different shapes. Some are brightly colored and look like pretty plants. The branching staghorn coral can only live in calm water because it is very delicate. The rounded brain coral can grow in rougher waters. The graceful sea fan is in no danger from the waves. It has a leathery skeleton which allows it to sway gently in the ocean currents.

crown-of-thorns starfish

Coral Reefs in Danger
The crown-of-thorns starfish is a threat to the life on a coral reef because it eats coral. This animal has already destroyed a quarter of the Great Barrier Reef. Some parts of the reef are entirely covered by feeding starfish. In one day a single starfish can destroy an area of coral twice as large as these two pages.

blue demoiselle fish

The clown fish is one fish that is not harmed by the sea anemone's sting. Its body produces a special liquid that stops the anemone releasing its poison. Clown fishes hide among the anemone's tentacles where they are safe from enemies.

staghorn coral

sea fan

butterfly fish

clown fish

anemone

brain coral

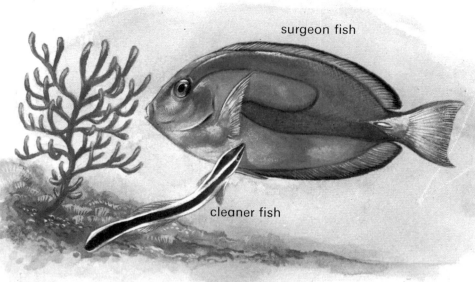
surgeon fish

cleaner fish

The cleaner fish does exactly what its name suggests. It cleans fish. It eats the small animals called parasites that live on other fishes' bodies. The surgeon fish gets its name from the sharp, knife-like spines just in front of its tail fin. When it is threatened, it lashes its tail from side to side, slashing its enemy's body.

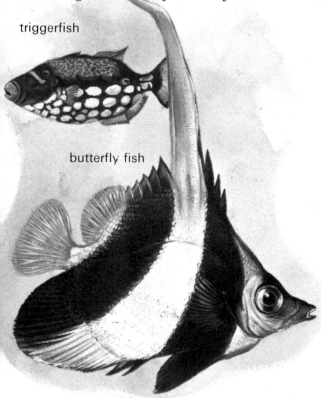
triggerfish

butterfly fish

Some of the most beautiful fishes of the coral reef are the butterfly fishes, or angel fishes. Most butterfly fishes have flat bodies with long fins. They are brightly colored, often with stripes or spots.

The triggerfish has an unusual way of protecting itself. When an enemy comes near, the fish raises a spike on its back. If the enemy is unwise enough to swallow the triggerfish, the spine catches in its throat. Usually the triggerfish pulls back its spine so that the fish can spit it out. But if the triggerfish cannot pull back its spine, it remains stuck in the enemy's throat and both fishes die.

The pearl fish shelters inside the body of a sea cucumber during the day. At night it comes out to search for small crustaceans to eat.

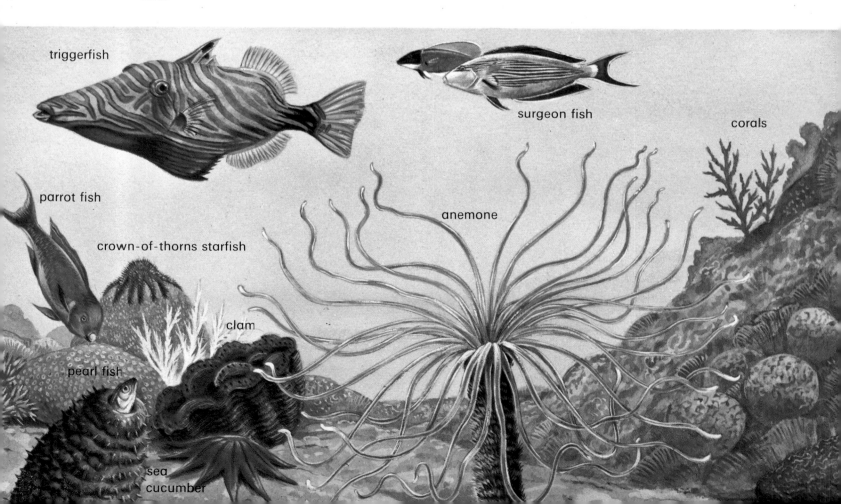
triggerfish

surgeon fish

corals

parrot fish

crown-of-thorns starfish

anemone

clam

pearl fish

sea cucumber

Shore Treasures

Making a collection of shells is fun and easy to do. You can add to your collection each time you visit a new seashore. The best time to search for shells is after a storm, when many shells that are normally found in deep water are thrown up onto the beach. Do not collect shells that still have living animals inside them.

When you get home, clean the shells in soapy water. You can then keep them in small boxes or glue them to a card. Make a label for each shell, writing down its name and where you found it. Try making pretty patterns with the shells. You can decorate boxes and jars with them. A good way to add to your collection is to trade shells with friends, especially with friends in foreign countries.

scallop
topshe
mussel
raz
cla
she
lim
dog whelk
periwin
cowrie

The highest point the tide reaches on the shore is called the strandline. Many interesting things are left along this stretch of beach when the tide goes out.

You may find rounded, lumpy "sponges" along the shore. These are the empty egg cases of the common whelk. A flat, white, oval "bone" about 5 inches (12 cm) long is probably the remains of the shell from inside a cuttlefish. It is called a cuttlebone.

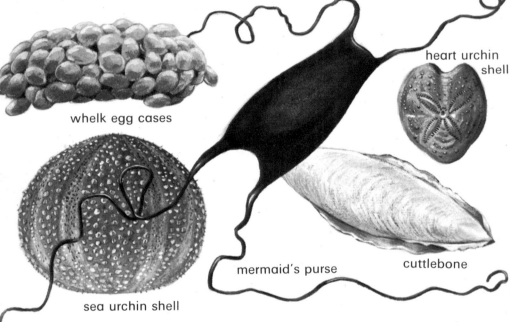

whelk egg cases

heart urchin shell

mermaid's purse

cuttlebone

sea urchin shell

Mermaid's purses are the empty cases in which dogfishes have laid their eggs. The long threads at each corner are usually broken off by the waves before the case reaches the shore. Urchin shells are all that remain of spiny sea urchins and heart urchins after they die. They are very brittle and break easily. If you find one, put it in cotton inside a box to keep it safe.

In the picture on the right are some of the seaweeds you may find along the shore. The little sacs of air on the bladder wrack and knotted wrack help them to float in the water. They are fun to pop when the seaweed is dry.

oarweeds

serrated wrack

bladder wrack

knott wrac

Index

In the picture below are some of the shore treasures washed up on a muddy beach. Also washed up is a plastic bottle and patches of oil. Rubbish and oil from ships at sea can kill animals and ruin the whole seashore.

sea kale

urchin shell

mermaid's purse

oil

razor clam shell

cuttlebone

jellyfish

whelk egg cases

limpet shell

lugworm casts